ULTIMATE CHRISTMAS DINING

FATHER CHRISTMAS AND FESTIVE TRADITIONS

Santa Claus, Father Christmas, St. Nicholas, and Sinterklaas are basically all the same person, descended from the Roman King of the Saturnalia. The original St. Nicholas was a fourth-century saint. His cult became popular in the Middle Ages, and in Switzerland, Germany, and the Netherlands he was linked with gift-giving on his feast day, December 6. The reindeer probably came from stories of the Norse god Woden who rode through the sky with reindeer and 42 ghostly huntsmen. Clement Moore's famous poem *A Visit from St. Nicholas* ("Twas the night before Christmas") sealed the image of Santa Claus, his reindeer, and the magical flying sleigh loaded with sacks of presents.

The image of a white-bearded man in a red and white suit is very recent. A century ago, Santa Claus was usually depicted in a long brown robe or furs carrying a cross and wine flask with a holly crown on his head. In 1885 a Boston printer, Louis Prang, first devised the red-suited Santa and this theme was later developed by the Coca-Cola advertising artist Haddon Sundblom in the 1930s, producing the modern image of a jolly character in a red suit trimmed with white fur.

Santa Claus
Santa started out in brown robes, but is recognized today by his red suit and white beard

CUSTOMS OLD AND NEW

There are endless games and pastimes, quaint customs, and odd traditions that happen only at this time of year. Many, such as the yule log, originated far in the past. To most people this is now a delicious log-shaped chocolate cake, but originally the yule log was dragged home from the woods with much ceremony and lit on Christmas

Eve to symbolize the sun and its warmth. An Englishman named Tom Smith invented the tube-shaped cracker, with a fire cracker inside to produce the bang. The paper hat in the cracker may be related to the hats worn in Tudor times by the Lords of Misrule, who were the leaders of the Christmas revels. Games, singing, and dancing were all seasonal entertainments and still are, albeit in very different forms. The singing of Christmas carols in the streets, a tradition imported into the US from England, began in Boston during the 1890s and soon spread throughout the country. Centuries ago in Europe, people gathered on the dark nights of the winter solstice and broke into merriment and wild behavior, fueled by ample food and drink. Not much changes! Pantomimes in England have a long tradition, and usually include role reversal of the sexes and of authority, and dressing up. The modern version can be traced through Saturnalian festivities and mumming plays to the 18th-century harlequinades.

Tree Baubles
Colored glass baubles are designed to catch the light

FOOD AND FEASTS

The concentration on food and feasting at Christmas is not surprising – before the days of canning and freezing, it was hard to survive the winter without stores of preserved food. Summer preserves and the last of the fresh food were brought out, while hardship was forgotten for a brief time of merrymaking. Some traditional recipes hark back to times when foods such as dried fruit and nuts were luxuries saved for feasting. Spices and flavorings are important in many recipes, echoing earlier dishes in which these precious ingredients were gathered from all over the known world. Most countries have dishes that are special to this time, such as the heavy fruit cake and round Christmas pudding from Britain, and the spiced cakes, cookies, and breads of central Europe.

Roast Turkey with Cornbread Stuffing
(See page 22 for recipe)
Serve with cranberries, blueberries, pumpkin, and roasted chestnuts

C hristmas is here,
 Merry old Christmas
Gift-bearing, heart touching,
Joy-bringing Christmas,
Day of grand memories,
 King of the year.

Washington Irving

If a young daughter or son, niece or nephew, or grandchild wants to help decorate the table don't discourage them because of their age – memories of time spent together will last far longer than a slightly imperfect centerpiece.

The Dining Table

Boisterous parties, extravagant feasts, or quiet suppers with friends and family focus the season's celebrations in a very special way. Usually there is at least one important meal that demands a beautifully presented table. Either work around the table settings you own, or choose a festive theme as a starting point. Then create a feast for the eyes with an exquisite candle centerpiece, decorated crockery, patterned table linen, and stunning homemade accessories.

Baroque Table Setting

Rich, opulent, and warm, in tones of claret and gold, this table setting is ideal for a sophisticated Christmas meal. A thick brocade cloth, silk napkins, and antique bone-handled cutlery are complemented by simple glass dishes and goblets decorated with gold paint. A festive arrangement of lilies and evergreen leaves presides over the table, and clusters of winter berries in gold-painted terra-cotta pots add the finishing touch.

Decorated Glass Bowl Ingredients

Sponge

Glass bowl

Red glass paint

Gold glass paint

◆ EQUIPMENT ◆

Mineral spirits
Soft cloth
Paint brush
Scissors
Dish for paint

Gold Filigree Goblet Ingredients

Gold outlining paint

Goblet

Sponge

Gold glass paint

◆ EQUIPMENT ◆

Mineral spirits
Soft cloth
Dish for paint
Scissors

ADDITIONAL LUXURIES
Fill brass bowls with chocolates and almonds wrapped in gold foil, and place thick cream candles in wooden candleholders painted matte gold. Tie napkins with strings of gold beads.

A warm and welcoming table is
the perfect setting for sharing
memories of the past, reading the
Christmas story, and other expressions
of holiday joy and thanksgiving for the
whole family.

DECORATING THE GLASS BOWL

Glass paints in rich jewel colors such as red and gold are ideal
for decorating glassware at Christmas. If you intend to use the
decorated items, choose durable nontoxic paints and avoid
painting areas that will come into contact with food.

A fine-tipped
paint brush
gives precision
when painting
tiny areas

*1 Prepare the glass surface for painting
by cleaning it carefully with mineral
spirits on a soft cloth.*

*2 Use a fine paint brush to apply red
glass paint to the underside of the
pattern on the rim of the bowl. Take
care not to smudge the paint onto the bowl
itself, but if you do, wipe it off quickly.*

Use a large sponge cut
down: the tiny holes
in a small sponge give
too dense a pattern

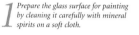

Dab the paint
gently onto
the glass

*3 Pour a small amount of gold paint
into a shallow dish or saucer.
Cut a small piece of sponge.*

*4 Dip the sponge into a little paint
and press it randomly onto the
underside of the bowl. Leave to dry.*

DECORATING THE GOBLET

The swirly gold pattern on this goblet is reminiscent of
traditional gold filigree work. Achieve the effect by applying
outlining paint straight from the tube to the outside
of the goblet and the rim of a plate.

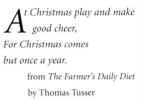

> *A t Christmas play and make
> good cheer,*
> *For Christmas comes*
> *but once a year.*
>
> from *The Farmer's Daily Diet*
> by Thomas Tusser

1 Prepare the glass surface for painting
by cleaning it carefully with mineral
spirits on a soft cloth.

2 Draw random swirls on the goblet
with outlining paint. Squeeze the tube
carefully to prevent blobs.

3 Draw lines on the base of the glass to
create a filigree-style pattern, taking
care not to make smudges.

4 Use a sponge to decorate the stem of
the glass with gold paint, following the
instructions for step 4 opposite.

Decorated Plate

Remove any grease marks from the plate with
a little mineral spirits on a soft cloth. Use a
tube of outlining paint to decorate the rim of
the plate in a style to match the goblet.

NATURAL TABLE SETTING

THE NATURAL MATERIALS AND EARTHY TONES of this fresh and stylish look lend themselves to a festive lunch. Dress the table up with gleaming brass and white china plates, lustrous gold glasses and wooden-handled cutlery, and echo the use of store-bought preserved and gold-sprayed oak leaves by adding a gold leaf motif to the linen tablecloth and napkins.

PRINTED TABLECLOTH Ingredients

Paper

Leaf

Tablecloth

• EQUIPMENT •

Pencil

Scissors

Kitchen knife

Paint brush

Towel

Potato

Gold fabric paint

GOLD LEAF NAPKINS Ingredients

Leaf

Paper

Napkin

Gold cord

• EQUIPMENT •

Pencil

Scissors

Pen

Needle and gold thread

Embroidery scissors

NATURAL BEAUTY
Adorn the table with a simple wreath of leaves and twigs, an ornamental cabbage, and napkins tied with brown string, gold thread, and oak leaves. Present each guest with a small gold trinket box decorated with a golden oak leaf.

*D*on't forget that the
smallest details often
require the greatest attention.

PRINTING THE TABLECLOTH

Cutting the potato into a square shape and using a tablecloth with a regular pattern such as checks or stripes will help you position the prints straight. Alternatively, choose a plain cloth and add an abstract pattern of prints.

Align the straight edges of the potato with the checks on the tablecloth to keep the print straight

1 Choose a suitable leaf, either fresh or preserved, to use as a guide. Place it on the paper, draw around it, and cut out.

2 Cut the potato in half and place the paper leaf on the flat edge. Cut around it with a kitchen knife.

3 Cut the potato into a rectangular shape around the leaf. Cut a detail such as a vein into the surface of the leaf.

4 Brush gold paint onto the cut leaf pattern, avoiding the carved-out detail.

5 Place an old towel or piece of fabric under the tablecloth, align the edges of the potato with the checks, and press it onto the cloth to print.

DECORATING THE NAPKIN

An oak-leaf motif outlined in gold cord on each napkin complements the prints on the tablecloth. Attach the motif with tiny gold stitches and decorate the napkins with oak leaves tied with brown string and gold thread.

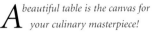

A beautiful table is the canvas for your culinary masterpiece!

1 Choose a leaf to use as a guide. Draw and cut out a paper leaf template as in step 1 opposite.

2 Draw around the paper template onto the napkin. Lay the gold cord around the leaf outline to measure how much will be needed and cut it.

Use embroidery scissors to fray tassels at the ends of the gold cord

Anchor the cord with tiny stitches in gold thread

3 Tie a knot near each end of the gold cord and fray the ends into tassels. Sew the cord around the leaf using gold thread.

4 When you reach the end of the gold cord, sew across both ends a few times to secure. Trim the tassels.

TARTAN TABLE SETTING

THE TRADITIONAL TARTAN look in holly green and berry red makes a classic evening setting for a Christmas Day or New Year's Eve feast. Soft chenille cloth, leaf green plates in textured wood and smooth china, green-handled cutlery, linen napkins, and chunky glass goblets are bathed in a rosy glow from two red candles, while homemade tartan crackers sit enticingly at each place setting.

FESTIVE CRACKERS Ingredients

One sheet patterned wrapping paper

Cardboard, 10 x 10in (25 x 25cm)

Gift

Paper hat

Snap

46in (117cm) ribbon

◆ EQUIPMENT ◆

Pencil

Ruler

Scissors

Sticky tape

Glue

Brown cardboard

String

Star name tag

LEAVES AND BERRIES
Continue the festive color scheme with a circular centerpiece of garden evergreens and glossy red and gold baubles on wire stems.

S ome of the most beautiful
table decorations are not
fashioned by hand but are the
result of Nature's handiwork.

MAKING THE CRACKER

Large and luxurious homemade Christmas crackers in a festive tartan print are extra-special when filled with carefully chosen gifts. Select a strong wrapping paper that will hold its shape when gathered at the ends of the cracker.

1 Draw a rectangle, 18 x 9¼in (45 x 23.5cm), on the wrapping paper and cut it out.

2 Cut a square, 8 x 8in (20 x 20cm), out of the cardboard and roll it into a tube, securing with tape.

3 Place the wrapping paper face down and lay the tube in the middle. Put the snap, gift, and hat inside the tube.

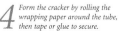

4 Form the cracker by rolling the wrapping paper around the tube, then tape or glue to secure.

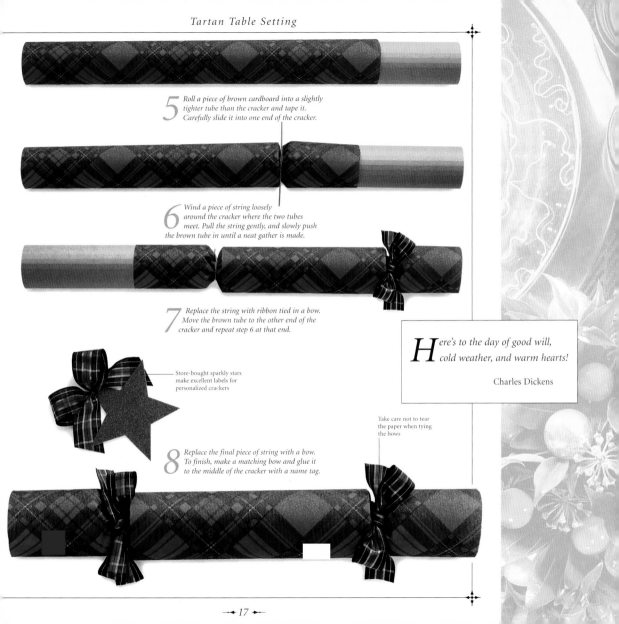

5 Roll a piece of brown cardboard into a slightly tighter tube than the cracker and tape it. Carefully slide it into one end of the cracker.

6 Wind a piece of string loosely around the cracker where the two tubes meet. Pull the string gently, and slowly push the brown tube in until a neat gather is made.

7 Replace the string with ribbon tied in a bow. Move the brown tube to the other end of the cracker and repeat step 6 at that end.

Store-bought sparkly stars make excellent labels for personalized crackers

Take care not to tear the paper when tying the bows

H ere's to the day of good will, cold weather, and warm hearts!

Charles Dickens

8 Replace the final piece of string with a bow. To finish, make a matching bow and glue it to the middle of the cracker with a name tag.

*F*ood prepared in a market's bakery and easily brought to the table will never give you the satisfaction gained from sweating over the details in your own kitchen.

CHRISTMAS FOOD

*Christmas would not be the same without
a celebration meal, complete with traditional
decorated cakes and cookies, but why not sample
the specialties of another country for a change?
Try elegant French oyster tarts as a starter;
roast goose or venison instead of turkey;
and strudel or pavlova for a memorable
Christmas dessert. Non-meateaters can enjoy
splendid dishes of salmon, trout, and carp, while
vegetarians will be impressed with a spectacular
delicacy stuffed with wild mushrooms.*

NORTH AMERICAN CHRISTMAS LUNCH

SINCE THE DAYS OF THE EARLY AMERICAN SETTLERS, roast turkey has been served as a celebration dish. Cornbread stuffing and a sweet-sour cranberry sauce are the usual accompaniments, other favorites being mashed potatoes flavored with garlic and herbs, stuffed onions, and creamed spinach. Special desserts include crunchy pecan pie, rich, sweet, and dark, and a creamy, tangy cheesecake topped with fresh blueberries.

There are few better ways to know that your meal has been a great success than if someone turns to you and asks "Do you mind if I get your recipe for…"

ROAST TURKEY WITH CORNBREAD STUFFING

INGREDIENTS
12lb (5.5kg) oven-ready turkey
1lb (500g) bacon
5–6 clementine shells filled with cranberries
and blueberries, slices of spiced, buttered
pumpkin, roasted chestnuts, and sage sprigs,
to garnish
CORNBREAD STUFFING
2 tbsp (30g) butter
3 onions, finely chopped
2 garlic cloves, chopped
6 celery stalks, chopped
⅛lb (250g) pork sausage meat
2 x 8½oz (240g) cans whole peeled chestnuts,
finely chopped
8oz (250g) cornbread, crumbled
1 tbsp each chopped fresh parsley, sage,
and thyme
salt and black pepper
1 tsp ground cinnamon
zest and juice of 1 orange
1 egg

ILLUSTRATED ON PAGES 20–21
ROAST TURKEY IS OFTEN SERVED IN NORTH AMERICA AT CHRISTMAS. CORNBREAD IS A FAVORITE STUFFING, AND QUITE DELICIOUS.

SERVES 6–8

1 To make the stuffing, melt the butter in a pan, add the onion, garlic, and celery, and cook for 2 minutes, stirring occasionally. Add the sausage meat and cook over high heat until lightly brown. Remove from the heat.

2 In a bowl, mix together the chestnuts, cornbread, parsley, sage, thyme, salt, pepper, cinnamon, orange zest, and juice. Add the sausage mixture. Stir until evenly blended, then mix in the egg.

3 Place a quarter of the stuffing in the neck end of the turkey, pull over the skin flap, and secure under the turkey using a trussing needle and string.

4 Fill the cavity of the turkey with the remaining stuffing, pull the skin over the

tail, and secure with the needle and string. Alternatively, make small stuffing balls.

5 Truss the turkey, using the needle and string to secure the wings and legs close to the body, and place in a roasting pan. Cover with bacon slices to keep the meat moist while cooking. Chill until ready to cook.

6 Preheat the oven to 375°F/190°C. Roast the turkey for 2 hours, then remove the bacon and cover with foil.

7 Return the turkey to the oven for 2 hours longer. Add stuffing balls 30 minutes before the end. To test for doneness, pierce with a sharp knife between the legs and body of the turkey – the juices should run clear.

8 Let the turkey stand for 20 minutes before removing the trussing string. Place on a warm serving dish and garnish with clementine shells filled with cranberries and blueberries, stuffing balls, if using, slices of spiced, buttered pumpkin, roasted chestnuts, and sage sprigs.

GARLIC & HERB POTATOES

INGREDIENTS
3lb (1.5kg) potatoes, peeled and cut into chunks
6 garlic cloves, peeled
salt and black pepper
2oz (60g) butter
2 fl oz (60ml) milk
2 tbsp chopped fresh parsley

ILLUSTRATED ON PAGE 20
IN AMERICA, SMOOTH, CREAMY, GARLIC-FLAVORED POTATOES ARE OFTEN SERVED WITH THE CHRISTMAS TURKEY

SERVES 6

1 Bring the potatoes and garlic to the boil in salted water. Cover and simmer gently for 10 minutes, or until the potatoes are tender.

2 Drain the potatoes and garlic, add pepper, butter and milk, and mash until smooth and creamy.

3 Stir in the parsley and pile on to a warm serving dish. Serve with roast turkey.

STUFFED ONIONS

INGREDIENTS
6 medium-sized white onions, peeled
2 tbsp olive oil
1 garlic clove, crushed
8oz (250g) wild mushrooms, chopped
2 tbsp chopped fresh oregano
salt and black pepper
2 tbsp fresh white bread crumbs
⅔ cup (150ml) vegetable stock
2 tbsp dry sherry
fresh parsley sprigs, to garnish

ILLUSTRATED ON PAGE 20
TRY THE MILD, SWEET FLAVOR OF WHITE ONIONS, FILLED WITH A MIXTURE OF WILD MUSHROOMS AND HERBS.

SERVES 6

1 Preheat the oven to 400°F/200°C. Place the onions in a pan of boiling water for 5 minutes, then drain well and cool.

2 Scoop out the center of each onion, leaving the base and shell intact. Finely chop the centers.

3 Heat the oil in a skillet and quickly cook the chopped onion, garlic, and mushrooms for 1–2 minutes, until tender. Stir in the oregano, salt, pepper, and bread crumbs.

4 Fill the cavity of each onion with the mushroom mixture. Place the remaining stuffing in an ovenproof dish and arrange the onions on top.

5 Pour the stock and sherry into the dish and bake for 30 minutes, or until the onions are tender. Arrange on a warm serving dish and garnish with parsley sprigs.

→ CRANBERRY SAUCE →

INGREDIENTS

1 cup (250ml) water
½ cup (125g) sugar
4 tbsp red currant jelly
1lb (500g) cranberries
zest and juice of 1 orange
1 cup (125g) walnuts, chopped (optional)

ILLUSTRATED ON PAGE 21
CRANBERRIES ARE ALWAYS SERVED WITH
ROAST TURKEY IN NORTH AMERICA. ADD
CHOPPED NUTS FOR EXTRA TEXTURE.

SERVES 6

1 Gently heat the water, sugar, and red currant jelly in a saucepan, stirring occasionally, until the sugar has dissolved.

2 Add the cranberries and bring to a boil. Simmer uncovered for 15 minutes. Stir in the orange zest and juice, and the walnuts, if using. Let cool.

3 Place in a serving dish, cover, and chill until required.

→ BLUEBERRY CHEESECAKE →

INGREDIENTS

1¼ cups (200g) all-purpose flour, plus extra for dusting
10 tbsp (150g) unsalted butter, cut into pieces
¼ cup (60g) sugar
1 egg yolk
FILLING
6 tbsp (90g) sugar
1lb (500g) cream cheese
1¼ cups (300ml) sour cream
2 eggs
1 tsp vanilla extract
finely grated zest of 1 orange
¾lb (375g) blueberries
2 tbsp red currant jelly
confectioners' sugar, to dust

ILLUSTRATED ON PAGE 21
THE MELT-IN-THE-MOUTH TEXTURE OF THE
SWEET PASTRY MAKES THIS
CHEESECAKE IRRESISTIBLE.

SERVES 6

1 Sift the flour into a bowl, add the butter, and rub in finely with the fingertips until the mixture resembles bread crumbs. Stir in the sugar and egg yolk and mix together to form a firm dough, adding a little cold water if necessary.

2 Roll out the dough on a lightly floured surface, thin enough to line the bottom and sides of a 1¾in (4.5cm) deep, 8½in (21cm) loose-bottomed fluted flan pan. Trim edges. Prick the bottom and chill for 30 minutes. Preheat the oven to 375°F/190°C.

3 Line the pastry shell with nonstick baking parchment and a thin layer of dried beans, rice, or pie weights. Bake blind in the preheated oven for 15 minutes, until the pastry is firm, but not brown. Remove the pastry shell from the oven and cool on a wire rack, still in the pan. Remove the paper, and

beans, rice, or pie weights, and reduce the heat to 300°F/150°C.

4 For the filling, place the sugar, cream cheese, cream, eggs, vanilla, and orange zest in a bowl and beat until smooth. Add one third of the blueberries to the mixture. Fold them in gently until evenly mixed.

5 Pour the mixture into the pastry shell and bake in the oven for 1 hour. Turn off the heat and allow the cheesecake to cool in the oven. When completely cool, release the pan and place the cheesecake onto a serving plate.

6 Melt the red currant jelly in a small saucepan and brush it over the top of the cheesecake. Arrange the remaining blueberries on top of the cheesecake and dust with confectioners' sugar to serve.

S ince ovens vary, baking times given for any recipe can only be used as a guide.

→ PECAN PIE →

INGREDIENTS

1¼ cups (150g) all-purpose flour, plus extra for kneading
¼ tsp salt
6 tbsp (90g) butter, cut into pieces
3 tbsp cold water
corn syrup, to brush
FILLING
4 eggs
1 cup (250ml) corn, golden, or maple syrup
6 tbsp (90g) unsalted butter, melted
1 tsp vanilla extract
2 cups (250g) pecans

ILLUSTRATED ON PAGE 21
THE RICH, NUTTY FLAVOR OF THIS PIE HAS
MADE IT A CLASSIC IN THE AMERICAN SOUTH.

SERVES 8–10

1 Sift the flour and salt into a bowl, add the butter, and rub in with the fingertips until it resembles bread crumbs. Stir in the water and mix to a firm dough with a fork.

2 Knead the dough on a lightly floured surface until smooth. Roll out and line the bottom and sides of a 9in (23cm) pie dish. Trim the edge, reroll the trimmings, and cut out 12 maple leaves with a leaf cutter. Brush

the leaves with water and position around the rim of the pie. Chill for 15 minutes. Preheat the oven to 400°F/200°C.

3 Line the pie shell with baking parchment and bake blind (see above) for 10 minutes. Remove the paper and pie weights and cool. Reduce heat to 350°F/ 180°C.

4 To make the filling, whisk the eggs, then slowly add the syrup, whisking to blend well. Whisk in the butter and vanilla and stir in the pecans. Spoon into the pie shell.

5 Bake for 40–45 minutes until risen, golden brown, and set in the center. Let cool, then brush with corn syrup to serve.

A German Christmas Dinner

THIS HEARTY SPREAD IS REMINISCENT OF MEDIEVAL BANQUETS. A rich, warming soup is followed by roast goose stuffed with apples and nuts, a popular feast dish that is served with red cabbage and potato dumplings. The apples and nuts are highly symbolic: apples represent the tree of knowledge, while nuts stand for the mystery of life. A spectacular coiled strudel makes a splendid dessert, followed by stollen, the fruit-filled bread always baked for Christmas.

Beef Soup with Noodles p.26 & left

Roast Goose with Apple Stuffing
p.26 & center
Potato Dumplings p.27 & right
Red Cabbage p.27 & center

Celebration Strudel p.27 & right
Stollen p.38 & right

I *have always thought of*
Christmas as a good time;
a kind, forgiving, generous, pleasant
time; a time when men and women
seem by one consent to open their
hearts freely; and so I say,
"God Bless Christmas."

Charles Dickens

→ Beef Soup with Noodles ←

Ingredients

2 tbsp vegetable oil
2lb (1kg) small beef bones
1lb (500g) shin of beef
2 chicken pieces (or a chicken carcass)
1 large onion, quartered
2 carrots, peeled and quartered
1 leek, sliced
4 celery stalks, sliced
1 bay leaf
½ tsp black peppercorns
½ tsp allspice berries
salt
3 quarts (3.5 liters) cold water
chopped fresh parsley

NOODLES

1 cup (125g) all-purpose flour, plus extra for
kneading
½ tsp salt
1 egg

ILLUSTRATED ON PAGE 24

THIS RICH, MEATY SOUP IS OFTEN SERVED ON
CHRISTMAS DAY IN GERMANY, FOLLOWED BY
ROAST GOOSE, HARE, OR VENISON.

SERVES 6

1 Heat the oil in a large pan. Add the bones,
beef, and chicken and brown evenly.
Alternatively, bake in a preheated oven at
400°F/200°C for 20 minutes, or until evenly
browned, then transfer to a pan.

2 Add the vegetables, bay leaf, peppercorns,
allspice, salt, and water to the pan. Bring
to a boil, cover, and simmer for 3 hours.

3 Meanwhile, make the noodles. Sift the
flour and salt into a bowl. Add the egg and
mix together, adding enough water to make
a firm dough.

4 Knead the dough on a lightly floured
surface until smooth, then wrap in plastic
wrap until required.

5 Strain the stock into a bowl and allow to
cool. Skim off the fat, return the stock to
the pan, and bring to a boil.

6 Roll the dough out until thin on a lightly
floured surface. Cut the dough into shapes
using a small star cutter. Drop the shapes
directly into the soup and return to a boil.
The noodles are cooked when they rise to the
surface. Divide the noodles equally among
individual plates and serve the soup hot,
sprinkled with chopped parsley.

→ Roast Goose with Apple & Nut Stuffing ←

Ingredients

8–10lb (4–5kg) oven-ready goose with giblets
salt and black pepper
6 slices goose fat or fatback
3 red apples, halved and cored
3 green apples, halved and cored
juice of 1 lemon
2 tbsp clear honey
1 cup (125g) toasted almonds, to garnish
fresh rosemary sprigs, to garnish

STUFFING

4 tbsp (60g) butter
1 cup (175g) raisins
4 onions, chopped
3 cooking apples, peeled, cored, and
coarsely chopped
1 cup (125g) blanched almonds, chopped
2¼ cups (250g) fresh white bread crumbs
1 tbsp each chopped fresh parsley, sage, and thyme
1 tsp ground cloves

ILLUSTRATED ON PAGES 24–25

GOOSE STUFFED WITH APPLES AND NUTS IS
THE TRADITIONAL CHRISTMAS DAY BIRD IN
GERMANY. THE USUAL ACCOMPANIMENTS ARE
RED CABBAGE AND POTATO DUMPLINGS.

SERVES 6–8

1 Preheat the oven to 400°F/200°C. Wipe
the goose and remove any excess fat from
inside. Place the giblets in a pan with water to
cover, and season. Bring to a boil, cover, and
simmer for 45 minutes. Reserve the stock for
gravy. Chop the liver for stuffing.

2 To make the stuffing, melt the butter and
cook the raisins, onion, and apple for 2–3
minutes, stirring. Remove from the heat and
add the almonds, bread crumbs, herbs,
cloves, and chopped liver.

3 Stuff the neck end of the goose, securing
the skin flap underneath the wing tips,
and place the remainder in the body cavity of
the goose or make stuffing balls. Secure the
tail end with skewers and truss the goose
neatly with string to hold the wings and legs
in position, close to the body.

4 Cover the breast with goose fat or fatback
and tie on securely with string. Sprinkle
with salt and pepper. Place a rack in a large
roasting pan and lay the goose breast side
down. Cook in the oven for 30 minutes, then
reduce the heat to 350°F/180°C.

5 Remove the goose from the oven and prick
the skin around the neck, wings, thighs,
back, and lower breast. Return to the oven for
3–3½ hours longer, removing excess fat and
basting regularly. Add stuffing balls 30
minutes from the end of the cooking time.

6 Test the goose by piercing the thigh with
a sharp knife – the juices should run pale
yellow, not pink. Let the goose rest for 15
minutes before carving.

7 Meanwhile, thinly slice the apple halves,
but not all the way through. Place each
half on a square of foil, drizzle with lemon
juice and honey, and add a sprig of rosemary.
Seal the parcels and bake in the oven for
10–15 minutes, then unwrap carefully.

8 Serve the goose garnished with the apples,
stuffing balls, if using, toasted almonds,
and sprigs of rosemary.

*I*t's wise to weigh out and
prepare all the ingredients in
a recipe before mixing them together.

POTATO DUMPLINGS

INGREDIENTS

2lb (1kg) medium-sized potatoes, scrubbed
salt and black pepper
¼ cup (30g) flour
2 tbsp (30g) semolina
1½ tsp freshly ground nutmeg
2 eggs, beaten
2 tbsp toasted bread crumbs

ILLUSTRATED ON PAGE 25
THESE LIGHT, FLUFFY DUMPLINGS ARE ONE
OF THE TRADITIONAL ACCOMPANIMENTS
FOR ROAST GOOSE.

MAKES 12

1 Boil the potatoes in salted water for about 10 minutes, until almost tender. Drain, leave until cool enough to handle, then peel.

2 Mix together in a bowl the flour, semolina, salt, pepper, and nutmeg.

3 Grate the potatoes coarsely and add to the bowl. Mix in lightly.

4 Add the eggs and mix together to form a soft dough, adding more flour if necessary. Using floured hands, shape the mixture into 20 round balls.

5 Cook the dumplings in boiling salted water for 8–10 minutes, or until they rise to the surface. Remove with a slotted spoon and drain on paper towels.

6 Arrange the dumplings on a warm serving plate and sprinkle with toasted bread crumbs, or roll them individually in the bread crumbs to coat evenly.

RED CABBAGE

INGREDIENTS

1 red cabbage, finely shredded
⅔ cup (150ml) red wine vinegar
2 tbsp (30g) sugar
1 tsp salt
4 whole cloves
1 bay leaf
2 tbsp (30g) goose fat or 2 tbsp vegetable oil
2 red onions, sliced
1 cooking apple, peeled, cored, and sliced
⅔ cup (150ml) giblet stock
4 tbsp red currant jelly
⅔ cup (150ml) red wine

ILLUSTRATED ON PAGE 24
SPICY SWEET AND SOUR RED CABBAGE IS A
FAVORITE WINTER DISH ALL OVER EUROPE. IT
IS A TRADITIONAL ACCOMPANIMENT TO ROAST
GOOSE, AND IS OFTEN COOKED IN GOOSE FAT.

SERVES 6

1 Place the cabbage, vinegar, sugar, salt, cloves, and bay leaf in a bowl and mix to blend evenly.

2 Heat the goose fat or oil in a flameproof casserole, add the onions and apple, and cook until lightly browned, stirring.

3 Stir in the cabbage and stock and bring to a boil. Cover and cook gently for about 30 minutes, until the cabbage is tender and most of the stock has evaporated. Add more stock or water if necessary.

4 Just before serving, stir in the red currant jelly and wine.

CELEBRATION STRUDEL

INGREDIENTS

6 tbsp (90g) unsalted butter, melted
13oz (400g) cream cheese
3 eggs, separated
¾ cup (175g) superfine sugar
1½ cups (175g) ground almonds
finely grated zest of 1 lemon
⅔ cup (125g) golden raisins
2 tsp ground cinnamon, plus extra for dusting
7oz (200g) phyllo pastry
confectioners' sugar, for dusting

ILLUSTRATED ON PAGE 25
STRUDEL CAN BE MADE IN MANY DIFFERENT
SHAPES AND SIZES, BUT THIS LARGE COIL IS
ONE OF THE MOST SPECTACULAR, AND IDEAL
FOR A SPECIAL OCCASION.

SERVES 6

1 Preheat the oven to 350°F/180°C. Line a large baking sheet with foil and brush with melted butter.

2 Place the cream cheese, egg yolks, and half the sugar in a bowl. Mix together with a wooden spoon, then beat until smooth. Stir in the ground almonds, lemon zest, raisins, and cinnamon until evenly blended.

3 Whisk the egg whites in a clean bowl until stiff, then gradually add the remaining sugar, whisking well after each addition. Add to the cheese mixture and fold in gently until evenly mixed.

4 Brush one sheet of phyllo pastry with butter, keeping the remainder covered with a damp dish towel. Cover with a second sheet and brush again.

5 Spread 1 tablespoon of filling along the pastry 1in (2.5cm) in from the long edge. Roll the pastry over the filling into a long roll.

6 Arrange the roll in a spiral, starting at the center of the baking sheet. Repeat with the remaining phyllo pastry, butter, and filling to make another 7 rolls, adding them onto the spiral to form a tight coil shape.

7 Brush the coil with melted butter and bake in the oven for 35–40 minutes, until crisp and brown. Meanwhile, fold the remaining pastry in half and brush with melted butter. Cut out 6 holly leaves and bake for 2 minutes. Dust the coil with confectioners' sugar and cinnamon and serve warm or cold, decorated with the holly leaves.

NORWEGIAN CHRISTMAS BUFFET

In Norway, the emphasis is on fresh, healthy ingredients, even at Christmas. The country's clear mountain streams produce some of the best fish in the world – hence the popularity of gravlax, the famous cured salmon. Tender lamb, bred on the high pastures, is cooked French-style on special occasions, with garlic and herbs, and the favorite dessert, a molded cream, is filled with seasonal berries, the preferred choice being the rare Arctic cloudberry.

Gravlax Salad p.30 & top left

Roast Lamb p.30 & center
Gratin Potatoes p.31 & bottom left
Caramelized Carrots & Onions p.31 & bottom right

Vanilla Cream Mold p.31 & right
Berry Sauce p.31 & top right

Good taste is not defined by excess, just as the meal that tastes good is not the result of excessive quantity.

GRAVLAX SALAD

INGREDIENTS
2 tbsp sea salt
1 tbsp sugar
2 tsp coarsely ground black pepper
½ cup (30g) finely chopped fresh dill
2lb (1kg) salmon fillets
cooked beets, mâche, and fresh dill sprigs
MUSTARD SAUCE
2 tbsp Dijon mustard
1 tbsp white wine vinegar
1 tbsp sugar
¼ cup (60ml) olive oil
1 tbsp chopped fresh dill

ILLUSTRATED ON PAGE 28
THIS NORWEGIAN SPECIALTY HAS A
DELICATE, PEPPERY FLAVOR.

SERVES 6

1 Mix the salt, sugar, and pepper in a bowl. Sprinkle a layer of the mixture over the bottom of a shallow glass dish. Sprinkle on some of the chopped dill and lay one salmon fillet on top, skin side down.

2 Sprinkle the fillet with more salt mixture and dill, then cover with a second fillet, skin side up, arranging them head to tail.

3 Repeat with the remaining fillets, ensuring they are layered skin next to skin and flesh next to flesh. Cover the dish with plastic wrap, place a board or plate on top, and weigh down with a few weights. Leave for 2–3 hours at room temperature, then refrigerate for 3–4 days, turning the fillets daily.

4 To make the mustard sauce, whisk the ingredients in a bowl until well blended.

5 Drain the salmon fillets, thinly slice, and arrange on a serving dish with strips of beets, mâche, and dill sprigs. Serve with the mustard sauce.

ROAST LAMB

INGREDIENTS
6–7lb (3–3.5kg) leg of lamb
5 whole garlic bulbs
sprigs of fresh rosemary, thyme, and parsley
salt and black pepper
2 tbsp clear honey
1 tbsp lemon juice
lemon wedges and fresh parsley sprigs,
to garnish

ILLUSTRATED ON PAGE 28–29
THIS CELEBRATION ROAST FROM NORWAY
SHOWS A DEFINITE FRENCH INFLUENCE, WITH
THE FLAVORS OF ROASTED GARLIC AND HERBS.

SERVES 6

1 Preheat the oven to 375°F/190°C. Place the leg of lamb in a roasting pan. Divide one garlic bulb into cloves and peel and slice the cloves.

2 Using a sharp knife, make small incisions all over the lamb. Insert alternate sprigs of herbs and slivers of garlic until the lamb is evenly covered.

3 Roast the lamb in the oven for 1¾ hours, then brush with the honey and lemon juice. Place the remaining garlic bulbs around the roast and cook for 30–40

minutes longer, until the lamb is tender and slightly pink inside.

4 Arrange on a serving dish and garnish with lemon wedges, parsley sprigs, and the bulbs of garlic, divided into cloves.

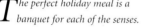

T he perfect holiday meal is a banquet for each of the senses.

CREAMED SPINACH

INGREDIENTS
3lb (1.5kg) spinach
SAUCE
1oz (30g) butter
1oz (30g) plain flour
salt and black pepper
¼ pint (150ml) milk
½ tsp freshly grated nutmeg
2 tbsp double cream

ILLUSTRATED ON PAGE 21
FRESHLY COOKED SPINACH IS SERVED
WITH A CREAMY SAUCE FLAVORED
WITH NUTMEG.

SERVES 6

1 Cook the spinach in ¼ pint (150ml) boiling water for 1 minute, then drain well and chop finely.

2 To make the sauce, place the butter, flour, salt, pepper, and milk in a small pan. Whisk continuously over a moderate heat until the sauce thickens.

3 Simmer the sauce over a low heat for 2 minutes, stirring occasionally. Add the nutmeg and spinach and stir until well blended and heated through.

4 Add the cream, stir well, and pour into a warm serving dish.

◆ GRATIN POTATOES ◆

INGREDIENTS
4 tbsp (60g) butter
2lb (1kg) potatoes, peeled
salt and black pepper
grated nutmeg
6oz (175g) Gruyère, grated
⅔ cup (150ml) light cream or milk
1 egg

ILLUSTRATED ON PAGE 28
THIS CREAMY POTATO DISH MAKES THE
PERFECT ACCOMPANIMENT TO A LARGE ROAST,
SUCH AS BEEF OR LEG OF LAMB.

SERVES 6

1 Preheat the oven to 375°F/190°C. Lightly butter a shallow, ovenproof dish.

2 Using a large grater or the slicer on a food processor, thinly slice the potatoes.

3 Arrange a layer of potato slices in the dish and sprinkle with salt, pepper, nutmeg, and a little grated cheese. Continue to layer the potatoes and cheese, reserving a little cheese for the top, until the dish is filled. Beat together the cream and egg and pour over the top of the dish.

4 Sprinkle the top with the reserved cheese. Bake for 40–50 minutes, or until the top is golden brown and the potatoes are tender.

◆ CARAMELIZED CARROTS & ONIONS ◆

INGREDIENTS
24 baby carrots, peeled
24 small onions
½ cup (125g) superfine sugar
¼ cup water
¼lb (125g) unsalted butter
1 tbsp lemon juice
1 tbsp chopped fresh parsley

ILLUSTRATED ON PAGE 29
CARAMELIZED VEGETABLES ACCOMPANY THE
CHRISTMAS ROAST IN NORWAY.

SERVES 6

1 Place the carrots and onions in separate pans of boiling salted water. Cover and simmer for 5–10 minutes, until tender. Drain and cool slightly, then peel the onions.

2 Gently heat the sugar and water, stirring occasionally, until the sugar has dissolved.

3 Boil rapidly until the bubbles subside and a golden brown syrup forms. Add the butter and stir to blend evenly, then stir in the lemon juice until smooth.

4 Place the carrots and onions in the caramel and toss to coat evenly. Place on a warm serving plate and sprinkle with chopped parsley. Serve hot.

◆ VANILLA CREAM MOLD ◆

INGREDIENTS
1 envelope gelatin
3 tbsp cold water
2½ cups (600ml) heavy cream
2 tsp vanilla extract
2 tbsp (30g) superfine sugar
1lb (500g) assorted fruit, such as strawberries,
raspberries, blueberries, and cherries
strawberry leaves, to decorate (optional)

ILLUSTRATED ON PAGE 29
THIS DELICATE CREAM FROM NORWAY IS IDEAL
TO FOLLOW A SUBSTANTIAL MAIN DISH.

SERVES 6

1 Place the gelatin and water in a small bowl over a pan of hot water and stir until the gelatin has dissolved.

2 Whisk the cream, vanilla extract, and sugar until well blended. Add the dissolved

gelatin and whisk until the mixture thickens. Pour the cream into a 3¾ cup (900ml) 7½in (19cm) ring mold and leave in the refrigerator for 3–4 hours to set.

3 Dip the mold in warm water and invert onto a serving dish. Fill the center with mixed berries and arrange berries around the bottom of the mold. Decorate with strawberry leaves and serve with Berry Sauce (see below).

◆ BERRY SAUCE ◆

INGREDIENTS
1 pint (250g) raspberries
1 pint (250g) strawberries
½lb (250g) blueberries
⅔ cup (150ml) water
2 tsp arrowroot
4 tbsp cherry brandy

ILLUSTRATED ON PAGE 29
USE ANY ASSORTMENT OF FRESH SOFT
FRUIT IN SEASON.

SERVES 6

1 Place the berries and water in a saucepan and bring to a boil. Cover and simmer for 5 minutes. Pour into a food processor and

blend until smooth, then strain, or press the fruit and juice through a sieve into a bowl.

2 Place the purée in a saucepan and bring to a boil. Blend the arrowroot with a little water until smooth. Add to the purée, stirring continuously until it comes back to a boil.

3 Simmer for 2 minutes, cool, and add the cherry brandy.

FESTIVE CAKES & COOKIES

THIS ENTICING COLLECTION OFFERS SOMETHING FOR EVERYONE, from a traditional English fruit cake, covered with royal icing, to the entrancing Scandinavian wreath cake, decorated with an intricate, interwoven pattern of marzipan fruit and leaves. An elegant pavlova, filled with frosted fruit and cream, strikes a lighter note. Other traditional offerings include rich chocolate truffles, shortbread, spiced cookies to hang on the tree, gingerbread men, and ginger pigs, tied with ribbons.

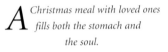

A Christmas meal with loved ones fills both the stomach and the soul.

FESTIVE CAKES & COOKIES

CHRISTMAS IS THE TIME FOR CELEBRATION CAKES. Rich, dark fruit cakes, redolent of wine and spices, are made well in advance and left to mature. Later, they can be covered with marzipan and lavishly iced. Fruit breads such as panettone, gingerbread, and other spiced cakes are also traditional fare.

Macaroon cake, a fairy castle made of meringue, or festive pavlova, piled high with frosted fruit, would make a stunning centerpiece. Shaped cookies, decorated with icing and tied with ribbons, can be hung on the tree to delight the children, while the grown-ups feast on chocolate truffles.

❖ TWELFTH NIGHT CAKE ❖

INGREDIENTS
½lb (250g) unsalted butter, softened, plus extra
for greasing
1 cup (250g) dark brown sugar
⅔ cup (150ml) port
⅔ cup (150ml) brandy
1½lb (750g) mixed dried fruit
4oz (125g) dried apricots, chopped
¼ cup (60g) mixed chopped peel
4oz (125g) glacé cherries, halved
1 tbsp grated orange zest
1 tbsp freshly squeezed orange juice
4 eggs
2 cups (250g) self-rising flour
1 tbsp ground mixed spice
¼ cup (90g) sliced almonds
DECORATION
3 tbsp apricot jam, boiled and sieved
1¼lb (900g) white marzipan
confectioners' sugar, for dusting
2 quantities royal icing (see opposite)
red and green food coloring
2yd (2m) red or green ribbons

ILLUSTRATED ON PAGE 33

TWELFTH NIGHT CAKE USED TO BE SPECIALLY MADE TO MARK THE FEAST OF EPIPHANY. IT WAS ALWAYS A RICH FRUIT CAKE COVERED WITH ALMONDS OR ALMOND PASTE, BUT BY THE 19TH CENTURY THE CAKE HAD BECOME A MASTERPIECE OF DECORATION, WITH PIPING AND GILDING FAR BEYOND MOST COOKS' CAPABILITIES. TODAY, IT IS SIMPLY A CHRISTMAS CAKE, COVERED WITH MARZIPAN AND ICING.

MAKES A 9IN (23CM) CAKE

1. Place the butter, sugar, port, and brandy in a large pan and bring to a boil. Stir in the mixed fruit, apricots, mixed peel, and cherries until well blended. Return to a boil and simmer very gently for 15 minutes. Cool the mixture overnight.

2. Lightly grease a 9in (23cm) round cake pan. Line the bottom and sides with a double thickness of nonstick baking parchment. Secure a double thickness strip of brown paper around the outside of the pan, then set the pan on a baking sheet lined with three to four layers of brown paper. Preheat the oven to 300°F/160°C.

3. Beat the orange zest and juice with the eggs. Sift the flour and spice into a large bowl and stir in the almonds. Add the beaten eggs and the cooled mixed fruit to the flour, stir until well mixed, then beat for 1 minute.

4. Place the mixture in the prepared pan, smooth the top, and bake in the oven for 3–3¼ hours, or until a skewer inserted into the center of the cake comes out clean. Cool in the pan.

5. Turn out the cake, leaving the lining paper in place. Wrap the cake securely in foil and store in a cool place for up to 3–4 months until ready to decorate.

DECORATING THE CAKE

1. Place the cake in the center of a cake board and brush with the apricot jam. Knead three quarters of the marzipan into a round, reserving the remainder. Roll out the marzipan on a surface lightly dusted with confectioners' sugar to form a round 3in (7cm) larger than the top of the cake.

2. Place the marzipan over the cake and smooth the top and sides with your hands. Trim off the marzipan at the base of the cake. Leave in a warm place to dry overnight.

3. Knead the trimmings and reserved marzipan together. Color a tiny piece red. Cut the remainder in half and color one piece light green and the other dark green. Roll out the dark green marzipan until thin and cut out holly leaves, using a small cutter. Roll out the light green marzipan and cut out ivy leaves, using a small cutter. Mold tiny berries with the red marzipan.

4. Make the royal icing (see opposite). Using a narrow spatula, spread the top of the cake with a thin, even layer of icing. Hold a long narrow spatula at a slight angle and draw it across the cake toward you in a continuous movement to make a smooth surface. Leave for 3–4 hours to dry.

5. Repeat with a second layer of icing and leave to dry. Spread the remaining icing smoothly over the side of the cake. Using a small narrow spatula, press into the surface of the icing on the side and pull away gently to form peaks. Let dry overnight.

6. Arrange the holly leaves and berries on top of the cake and secure with a little icing. Fit the ribbon around the cake and the cake board and secure with a little icing. Leave in a cake pan in a warm dry place to set overnight. If uncut, the cake will keep in a tin for up to 1 year.

PANETTONE

INGREDIENTS
3½ cups (450g) unbleached all-purpose flour,
plus extra for dusting
1 tsp salt
3 tbsp (45g) superfine sugar
2 envelopes quick-rise dry yeast
¼lb (125g) unsalted butter, melted
⅔ cup (150ml) milk
1 tsp vanilla extract
1 egg, plus 2 yolks
vegetable oil, for brushing
1 tbsp butter, plus extra for greasing
½ cup (125g) glacé fruits
½ cup (90g) golden raisins
2 tsp grated lemon zest
confectioners' sugar, for dusting

THIS LIGHT, AIRY CAKE IS THE ITALIAN
VERSION OF CHRISTMAS CAKE.

SERVES 6–8

1 Sift the flour, salt, sugar, and yeast into a
warm mixing bowl, or food processor
fitted with a dough beater.

2 Add the melted butter to the milk. Beat in
the vanilla, egg, and yolks. Mix into the
flour to form a soft dough. Knead for 8–10
minutes, or 2–3 minutes in a food processor,
until smooth and elastic. Brush with oil,
cover with plastic wrap, and leave in a warm
place for 1–2 hours, until doubled in size.

3 Meanwhile, lightly grease a 6in (15cm)
round cake pan and line the bottom with
nonstick baking parchment. Dust the inside
with flour. Set the pan on a baking sheet and
tie a piece of foil around the outside of the
pan to stand 3in (7cm) above the rim.

4 Knead the dough for 1–2 minutes, until
smooth, then roll out into a flat round.
Mix together the glacé fruits, raisins, and
lemon zest, scatter over the surface of the
dough, and press in with the rolling pin.

5 Knead the dough until smooth. Gather
into a ball and cut a cross in the top with
scissors. Place in the cake pan, cover carefully
with oiled plastic wrap, and leave in a warm
place to rise until the center touches the
wrap. Preheat the oven to 400°F/200°C.

6 Remove the plastic wrap, recut the cross,
and place the tablespoon of butter in the
center. Bake for 10 minutes, then lower the
heat to 350°F/180°C and bake for 40–45
minutes, until a skewer inserted into the
center comes out clean. Cool in the pan for
10 minutes, remove the foil, and ease the cake
out of the pan. Cool on a wire rack. Dust
with confectioners' sugar before serving.

WREATH CAKE

INGREDIENTS
¾ cup (90g) almonds, chopped
½ cup (90g) golden raisins
½ cup (90g) dark raisins
½ cup (90g) glacé cherries, halved
¼ cup (60g) mixed chopped peel
1⅓ cups (175g) self-rising whole wheat flour
1 tsp ground cardamom
1 cup (175g) moist light brown sugar
12 tbsp (175g) unsalted butter, softened, plus
extra for greasing
3 eggs
3 tbsp apricot jam, boiled and sieved
1¼lb (750g) white marzipan
dark green food coloring
confectioners' sugar, for dusting
marzipan apples, pears, and oranges and holly
and ivy leaves (see page 38), to decorate
2 tbsp royal icing (see below)

ILLUSTRATED ON PAGE 33
THIS SCANDINAVIAN CAKE MAKES A STUNNING
CENTERPIECE FOR THE CHRISTMAS TABLE.

SERVES 10

1 Preheat the oven to 300°F/160C°. Grease a
9in (23cm) ring mold and place a circle of
nonstick baking parchment on the bottom.

2 Mix together the almonds, golden raisins,
dark raisins, cherries, mixed peel, and
sherry.

3 Sift the flour and cardamom into a bowl
and add the sugar, butter, and eggs. Mix
well, then beat for 2–3 minutes, until smooth
and glossy. Fold the fruit and nuts into the
mixture until evenly distributed.

4 Place the mixture in the pan, smooth the
surface, and cook in the oven for 1 hour–
1 hour 10 minutes, until the cake feels firm to
the touch. Test by inserting a skewer into the

center of the cake – it should come out clean.
Allow the cake to cool in the pan, then invert
onto a wire rack and remove the paper.

5 Brush the cake evenly with the apricot
glaze. Color the marzipan leaf green and
knead until evenly colored. Roll out on a
surface dusted with confectioners' sugar to
form a round 2in (5cm) larger than the cake.
Cut a small circle out of the center, then place
the marzipan over the center of the ring.

6 Ease the marzipan around the inside of
the cake and smooth over the top and
down the sides, trimming off the excess at the
base. Place the cake on a cake board or plate,
store in a box or tin with a lid, and leave in a
warm dry place to set overnight.

7 Arrange the marzipan fruit and leaves
evenly over the cake, bending the leaves
to shape. Use a little royal icing to make
them stick firmly.

ROYAL ICING

INGREDIENTS
2 egg whites
¼ tsp lemon juice
4 cups (500g) confectioners' sugar, sieved
1 tsp glycerin

MAKES ENOUGH TO COVER A 6IN (15CM) CAKE

1 Stir the egg whites and lemon juice in a
bowl. Mix in enough confectioners'
sugar to give the consistency of unwhipped cream.

2 Add the remaining sugar a little at a time,
gently beating after each addition, until

the icing is smooth and stands in soft peaks.
Stir in the glycerin until well blended. Place
in an airtight container, or cover the bowl
with a damp dish towel until ready to use.
WARNING: RAW EGGS CAN TRANSMIT
SALMONELLA. AVOID SERVING TO THE ELDERLY,
YOUNG CHILDREN, AND PREGNANT WOMEN.

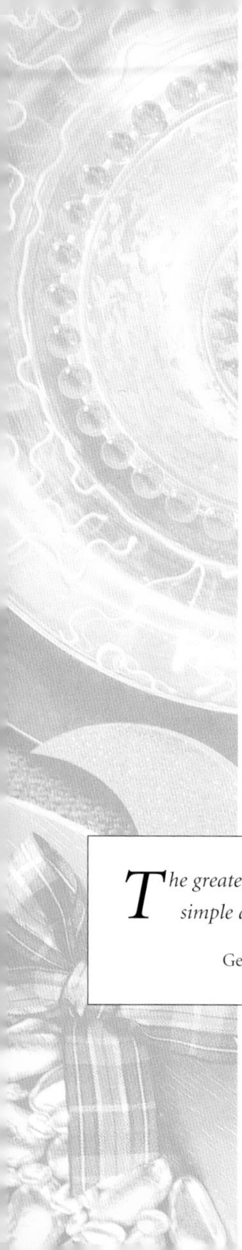

❧ Polish Spiced Cake ❧

Ingredients
1 tbsp melted butter
1 tbsp fresh white bread crumbs
½ lb (250g) butter
1 cup (250g) superfine sugar
¼ cup (60ml) water
3 eggs, separated
2 cups (250g) self-rising flour
1½ tsp ground mixed spice
2 tbsp (30g) chopped angelica
2 tbsp (30g) mixed chopped peel
¼ cup (60g) glacé cherries, chopped
½ cup (60g) walnuts, chopped
confectioners' sugar, for dusting
fresh holly, to decorate

THE MOST IMPORTANT HOLIDAY OF THE YEAR IN POLAND IS NEW YEAR'S EVE. SPICED CAKE IS ALWAYS SERVED, PREFERABLY WITH VODKA.

Serves 6–8

1 Preheat the oven to 350°F/180°C. Brush an 8in (20cm), 6 cup (1.5 liter) fluted ring mold with melted butter and coat with bread crumbs.

2 Place the butter, sugar, and water in a saucepan and heat gently, stirring occasionally, until melted. Bring to a boil, boil for 3 minutes until syrupy, then allow to cool.

3 Place the egg whites in a clean bowl and whisk until they stand in stiff peaks.

4 Sift the flour and mixed spice into a bowl, add the angelica, mixed peel, cherries, and walnuts and mix well. Stir in the egg yolks.

5 Pour the cooled syrup into the flour mixture and beat with a wooden spoon to form a soft batter. Using a plastic spatula, gradually fold in the egg whites until the mixture is evenly blended.

6 Pour the mixture into the prepared mold and lightly smooth the surface. Bake in the preheated oven for 50–60 minutes, or until the cake springs back when pressed in the center. Turn out and cool on a wire rack. To serve, dust thickly with confectioners' sugar and decorate with a sprig of holly.

❧ Norwegian Macaroon Cake ❧

Ingredients
1lb (500g) ground almonds
2 tbsp (15g) flour
2½ cups (500g) superfine sugar
1 tbsp finely grated lemon zest
1 tsp almond extract
3 egg whites, whisked
ICING
1 tsp orange-flower water
1 egg white
2 cups (250g) confectioners'
sugar, sifted
DECORATION
fresh fruit and bay leaves
confectioners' sugar,
for dusting

ILLUSTRATED BELOW

THIS CAKE IS A FAVORITE FOR BIRTHDAY, WEDDING, AND CHRISTMAS CELEBRATIONS. WARNING: RAW EGGS CAN TRANSMIT SALMONELLA. AVOID SERVING TO THE ELDERLY, YOUNG CHILDREN, AND PREGNANT WOMEN.

Serves 20

1 Preheat the oven to 375°F/160°C. Line three or four baking sheets with nonstick baking parchment.

2 Mix together the ground almonds, flour, sugar, lemon zest, and almond extract in a bowl until evenly blended.

3 Gradually stir in enough egg white to form a soft but firm dough. Divide into manageable pieces and roll out each piece into a rope as thick as a finger.

4 To construct the cake, the "ropes" are cut into 12 graduated lengths, and formed into circles. Start by cutting a piece 4in (10cm) long. Form into a circle, pressing the ends together to join neatly, and place on a baking sheet.

5 Continue to cut lengths and make circles, increasing the length by 1in (2.5cm) each time, until there are 12 graduated circles in total, the largest measuring 15in (37.5cm) in circumference.

6 Bake the circles in batches for 20 minutes, until pale brown and firm. Let cool for 10 minutes, then slide onto a wire rack.

7 To make the icing, whisk the orange-flower water and egg white in a bowl. Gradually add the confectioners' sugar, beating well after each addition, until it is the consistency of thick cream. Continue to beat and add sugar until it stands in soft peaks.

8 Spoon the icing into a waxed paper pastry bag fitted with a No. 1 plain writing nozzle. Alternatively, snip the point off the end of the bag, half-fill with icing, and fold down the top.

9 Using a flat cake plate or a cake board, place the largest circle in the center. Spread with a little icing and place the next largest circle on top. Repeat until all the circles are stacked together. Pipe fine threads of icing in loops around each ring until evenly covered. Decorate the base and top with fresh fruit and bay leaves and dust with confectioners' sugar.

*T*he greatest dishes are very simple dishes.

George Auguste Escoffier

✦ PAVLOVA ✦

INGREDIENTS

5 egg whites
1¼ cups (290g) superfine sugar,
plus extra for frosting
½ tsp vanilla extract
1½ tsp vinegar
1½ tsp cornstarch
3oz (90g) white seedless grapes
3oz (90g) red seedless grapes
8 physalis, optional
3oz (90g) cherries
3oz (90g) strawberries
1¼ cups (300ml) heavy cream
⅔ cup (150ml) plain yogurt
½ cup (125g) mixed glacé fruits, chopped

ILLUSTRATED ON PAGE 32
THE LIGHT CRISP MERINGUE WITH A
WHIPPED CREAM CENTER WAS NAMED IN
HONOR OF THE RUSSIAN PRIMA BALLERINA,
ANNA PAVLOVA. THIS FESTIVE VERSION IS
DECORATED WITH FROSTED FRUIT.

SERVES 6

1 Preheat the oven to 275°F/140°C. Line a baking sheet with nonstick baking parchment and draw a 9in (23cm) circle in the center. Turn the paper over.

2 Place 4 egg whites in a clean bowl. Beat by hand or with an electric beater until the whites are stiff. Gradually add the sugar, whisking well after each addition, until the meringue is thick.

3 Blend together the vanilla extract, vinegar, and cornstarch in a bowl and add to the meringue. Whisk until the meringue is thick and glossy and stands up in soft peaks.

4 Spoon the meringue into a large nylon pastry bag fitted with a large star nozzle. Pipe a ring of shells following the marked line. Fill in the center with a coil of meringue.

5 Pipe another ring of shells on top of the first ring and fill in the center with the remaining meringue. Alternatively, spread the remaining meringue inside the circle and smooth the top.

6 Bake in the oven for 1 hour, then turn off the heat and leave the pavlova for 2–3 hours to become cold, without opening the oven door. Store in an airtight container for up to 2 weeks, or until required.

7 Whisk the remaining egg white in a bowl. Place some superfine sugar in a bowl and line a wire rack with paper towels.

8 Cut the white and red grapes into small bunches, brush all over with egg white, then dip into the superfine sugar until coated evenly. Place on the paper-covered rack and leave in a warm place to dry. Frost the physalis, if using, the cherries, and the strawberries in the same way.

9 Whip the cream and yogurt in a bowl until just thickened. Add the glacé fruit and fold in gently. Spoon the fruit and cream into the center of the pavlova and decorate with the frosted fruit.

✦ MINCE PIES ✦

INGREDIENTS

3 cups (375g) all-purpose flour, plus extra for
dusting
12 tbsp (175g) butter
2 tbsp (30g) sugar
1 egg yolk
12oz (375g) mincemeat
confectioners' sugar, to dust

THIS RECIPE DATES BACK TO MEDIEVAL TIMES.
MINCEMEAT WAS ORIGINALLY A MIXTURE
OF SHREDDED OR MINCED MEAT, DRIED FRUIT,
AND SPICES – HENCE THE NAME – AND THE
MINCE PIE WAS LIKE A MODERN MEAT PIE.
SINCE THEN THE RECIPE HAS BECOME
SWEETER, AND THE MEAT HAS DISAPPEARED.

MAKES 20

1 Preheat the oven to 400°F/200°C. Sift the flour into a bowl, add the butter, and rub in lightly with the fingers until the mixture resembles bread crumbs.

2 Using a fork, stir in the sugar, egg yolk, and enough cold water to form a soft dough. Knead gently on a lightly floured surface.

3 Roll out the pastry until thin and cut out 20 x 3in (7cm) rounds and 20 x 2in (5cm) rounds, using fluted cutters. Knead the trimmings together and reroll as necessary.

4 Dust 20 x 3in (7cm) tartlet pans with flour and line with the larger pastry circles. Prick the bottom of each with a fork and half-fill with mincemeat. Brush the edges of each smaller circle with water, invert, and press on top of each tart to seal the edges.

5 With the point of a knife, pierce a hole in the center of each tart lid to allow the steam to escape. Bake in the preheated oven for 15–20 minutes, until light brown. Cool on a wire rack before removing from the pans. Dust with confectioners' sugar before serving.

STOLLEN

INGREDIENTS

¼ cup (60g) raisins
¼ cup (60g) currants
¼ cup (60g) candied citrus peel, chopped
¼ cup (60g) glacé cherries, halved
2 tbsp (30g) angelica, chopped
3 tbsp dark rum
3 cups (375g) unbleached all-purpose flour, plus extra for kneading
¼ tsp salt
2 envelopes quick-rise dry yeast
6 tbsp (90g) superfine sugar
1 tsp grated lemon zest
¼ tsp almond extract
½ cup (125ml) milk, warmed
2 eggs
¼lb (125g) unsalted butter, softened
¼ cup (30g) sliced almonds
confectioners' sugar, for dusting

ILLUSTRATED ON PAGE 25
WRAPPED IN FOIL OR PLASTIC WRAP, THIS GERMAN FRUIT BREAD WILL KEEP FOR 1 MONTH.

SERVES 12

1 Mix the raisins, currants, peel, cherries, angelica, and rum in a bowl. Cover and leave for several hours. Drain, reserving the rum. Sift the flour and salt into a warm bowl. Stir in the yeast, half the sugar, and the lemon zest.

2 Place the almond extract, warm milk, eggs, and reserved rum in a separate bowl. Whisk until blended and add to the flour with 6 tablespoons (90g) of the butter. Mix with a wooden spoon and beat until smooth.

3 Turn the dough out onto a floured surface and knead until smooth. Melt the remaining butter. Place the dough in a bowl. Brush bowl and dough with the butter, cover with plastic wrap, and leave for 30 minutes. Knead until smooth, return to the bowl, and cover. Place in a warm spot until doubled in size, 1–2 hours.

4 Turn out the dough, punch it down to remove air bubbles, and knead into a round. Flatten it to a thickness of ½in (1cm). Sprinkle the soaked fruit and the almonds over the surface, then gather up the dough and knead lightly to distribute the fruit. Roll out to form a 12 x 8in (30 x 20cm) oblong.

5 Brush with butter and sprinkle with the remaining sugar. Fold one end into the middle and press down. Bring the opposite side over the fold. Using floured hands, press down the ends and taper them slightly.

6 Line a jelly roll pan with nonstick baking parchment. Place the loaf on the pan and brush with melted butter. Cover loosely with a dish towel and leave until doubled in size, about 30 minutes. Preheat the oven to 375°F/190°C. Bake for 30–40 minutes, until golden brown. Cool on a wire rack and dust with confectioners' sugar to serve.

ST. NICHOLAS SPICE COOKIES

INGREDIENTS

2 cups (250g) self-rising flour
¼ tsp of each ground spice: cinnamon, nutmeg, anise, mace, cloves, cardamom, and ginger
½ cup (125g) light brown sugar
½ cup (60g) ground almonds
¼lb (125g) unsalted butter, softened
1 egg, beaten
½ cup (60g) sliced almonds
2 tbsp (30g) currants
1 recipe royal icing (see page 175)
red, yellow, and green food coloring
24 x 6in (15cm) lengths of thin colored ribbon

ILLUSTRATED ON PAGE 32
THESE COOKIES ARE TRADITIONAL IN HOLLAND.

MAKES 24

1 Preheat the oven to 375°F/190°C. Line 3–4 baking sheets with nonstick baking parchment or waxed paper.

2 Sift the flour and spices into a bowl. Stir in the sugar, ground almonds, and the butter, cut into small pieces. Rub in with the fingers until the mixture resembles fine bread crumbs. Stir in just enough egg to bind the mixture together. Knead into a neat ball.

3 Roll out the dough until thin, and cut out shapes using a gingerbread man cutter or other cutters. Place the cookies on the baking sheets and decorate the gingerbread men with sliced almonds or currants. To make hanging decorations, make a hole at the top of each shape with a drinking straw. Bake for 10–15 minutes until golden brown. Cool on the baking sheet, then transfer to a wire rack.

4 Divide the royal icing into 3 portions and color them red, yellow, and green. Spoon each color into a waxed paper pastry cone, fold down the top, and snip off the point.

5 Outline some of the shapes with a line of icing, and fill in the shapes with lines and dots, varying the colors. Let dry in a cool place. Use colored ribbons to hang some of the cookies on the Christmas tree.

MARZIPAN FRUIT

INGREDIENTS

8oz (250g) white marzipan
green, yellow, and orange food coloring
whole cloves, cut in half crosswise

DECORATE CAKES, OR THE CHRISTMAS TABLE, WITH THIS ASSORTMENT OF FRUIT.

MAKES 40

1 Divide the marzipan into 4 pieces. Color 2 pieces light and dark green; color the remainder yellow and orange.

2 Using pea-sized pieces, mold the light green, orange, and yellow marzipan into apple, orange, and pear shapes. Texture the oranges by rubbing gently on a fine grater. Insert a clove top into each fruit as a stalk, and the end as a calyx.

3 Using the dark green marzipan and a small leaf cutter, cut out holly, ivy, and grape leaves. Mark the veins by pressing a real leaf onto the marzipan leaf, then bend the leaves into shape.

4 Let dry in a warm place overnight. To decorate a cake, use a little icing to hold the shapes in position.

GINGER PIGS

INGREDIENTS

1¼ cups (175g) self-rising flour,
plus extra for dusting
1 tsp ground ginger
1 tsp nutmeg
finely grated zest of 1 lemon
½ cup (90g) soft brown sugar
¼ lb (125g) unsalted butter
⅓ cup (60g) currants
1 egg, beaten
60 x 12in (30cm) lengths of thin colored ribbon

ILLUSTRATED ON PAGE 32
THESE CORNISH GINGER COOKIES ARE
BAKED IN MANY SHAPES — STARS, HEARTS, AND
GINGERBREAD MEN, AS WELL AS PIGS — TO
DISPLAY IN SHOPS AND MARKETS DURING
ADVENT, TIED WITH FESTIVE RIBBON.

MAKES 60

1 Sift the flour and spices into a bowl. Stir
in the lemon zest and sugar. Rub in the
butter finely with the fingers.

2 Add 3 tablespoons (45g) of the currants
and the egg and mix to form a firm
dough. Knead on a lightly floured surface
until smooth. Wrap in plastic wrap and chill
for 1 hour.

3 Line 2 baking trays with nonstick baking
parchment or waxed paper and preheat
the oven to 375°F/190°C.

4 Roll out the dough on a lightly floured
surface until ¼in (5mm) thick. Using a
pig-shaped cutter, or other cookie cutter, cut
out about 60 shapes, kneading and rerolling
the trimmings when necessary.

5 Arrange the shapes far apart on the baking
sheets, press a currant in position for each
eye, and bake in the oven for 10–15 minutes.
Let cool on the sheet for 10 minutes, then
transfer to a wire rack.

6 Tie each "pig" cookie around the neck with
colored ribbon, and arrange on a serving
plate, or tie onto the Christmas tree.

SCOTTISH SHORTBREAD

INGREDIENTS

1¼ cups (175g) all-purpose flour,
plus extra for dusting
4 tbsp (60g) superfine sugar,
plus extra for sprinkling
½ cup (60g) cornstarch or ground rice
¼ lb (125g) unsalted butter, diced

ILLUSTRATED ON PAGE 33
SCOTTISH SHORTBREAD IS TRADITIONALLY
SHAPED IN WOODEN MOLDS AND CUT INTO
TRIANGLES CALLED "PETTICOAT TAILS."

MAKES 12

1 Preheat the oven to 325°F/160°C. Mix
together 1 teaspoon each of flour and
sugar and use to dust a 4in (10cm)
shortbread mold, if available. If not, use 4in
(10cm) cookie cutters. Line a baking sheet
with waxed paper.

2 Sift the flour, cornstarch, and sugar into a
mixing bowl. Rub in the butter finely with
your fingers until the mixture begins to hold
together. Knead into a firm dough.

3 Cut the dough into 12 pieces. Roll out one
piece on a lightly floured surface to the
size of the mold, if using. Place the dough
in the mold and press to fit neatly. Using a
narrow spatula, trim off the excess dough.
Invert onto the baking sheet and tap firmly to
release the shape. Repeat with the remaining
dough, reflouring the mold each time.

4 If not using a mold, roll out the dough on
a floured surface to a thickness of ¼in
(5mm) and cut out 12 shapes with cookie
cutters. Bake in the oven for 35–40 minutes
until pale in color.

5 Sprinkle the top of the shortbread with a
little sugar and let cool on the baking
sheet.

CHOCOLATE TRUFFLES

INGREDIENTS

½ cup (125ml) heavy cream
2 tbsp dark rum, brandy, or sherry
½lb (250g) white, baker's semisweet, or
milk chocolate, melted and cooled
COATINGS
2 tsp cocoa
1 tsp confectioners' sugar
2oz (60g) white or baker's semisweet
chocolate, grated
2 tbsp chocolate sprinkles or chopped nuts

ILLUSTRATED ON PAGE 33
CHOCOLATE TRUFFLES ARE ALWAYS A FAVORITE
AT CHRISTMASTIME. PACK THEM INTO PRETTY
BOXES AS A GIFT, OR PILE THEM HIGH ON A
DECORATIVE PLATE.

MAKES 30

1 Place the cream in a pan, bring to a boil to
sterilize, then cool until warm. Stir in the
rum, brandy, or sherry when the mixture is
lukewarm, then add it to the cool, melted
chocolate, stirring until evenly blended.

2 Beat the mixture until light and fluffy,
then chill for 2–3 hours until it is firm
enough to divide into portions.

3 Using a teaspoon, scoop out balls of the
mixture onto a tray lined with paper
towels, keeping them about 1in (2cm) apart.
Chill until firm, about 1 hour, then roll each
portion of truffle mixture into a neat ball.

4 Sift the cocoa and confectioners' sugar
together on a plate and roll some of the
truffles in the mixture to coat evenly. Repeat,
coating the remaining truffles in grated
chocolate, chocolate sprinkles or nuts.
Chill until set.

Acknowledgments

C.R.Gibson®
FINE GIFTS SINCE 1870

This book is based on *Ultimate Christmas*, first published in Great Britain in 1996 by Dorling Kindersley Limited, London

Copyright © 2000 Dorling Kindersley Limited, London
Ultimate Christmas text copyright © 1996 Jane Newdick

All rights reserved under International and Pan-American Copyright Conventions. No part of this publication may be reproduced, stored in an retrieval system, or transmitted in any form or by any means, electronic, mechanical, photocopying, recording or otherwise, without the prior written permission of the copyright owner.

Developed by Matthew A. Price, Nashville, Tennessee.

Published by C. R. Gibson®
C. R. Gibson® is a registered trademark of Thomas Nelson, Inc.
Norwalk, Connecticut 06856

Printed in China by South China Printing

ISBN 0–7667–6758–2
UPC 082272–46688–3
GB4155

Picture Credits

Photography by Dave King, except: Martin Brigdale 18–21, 22(t), 23(t), 24–25, 26(t), 28–29, 30(t), 32–33, 36–39